Purple Ronnie's Guide to Life

Published in 1992 by Statics (London) Ltd,
41 Standard Road, London NW10 6HF
Tel: 081-965 3327

© 1992 Giles Andreae
ISBN 1-873922-03-5
Print origination by Diva Graphics Ltd.
Printed in England by HPH Print Ltd,
8 Gorst Road, London NW10 6LE

Words by Giles Andreae
and Simon Andreae
Pictures by Janet Cronin
and Giles Andreae

Contents

Life

Life is a sort of a person machine
That fits in a hole in your tummy
And privately tickles your laughing device
When somebody says something funny

Life is the bit that goes droopy and flat
Whenever you're lonely or sad
And somersaults round in the top of your head
When you're in love or just glad

Most of the time it just jiggles around
But when you're asleep in your bed
It goes on adventures in dangerous lands
And feeds them back into your head

Once when it thought I was sleeping
I secretly opened my eyes
And just caught a glimpse of it climbing back in
With cowboys and pirates and spies

What is Life?

Everything that moves has a life inside it and the Life is the bit that makes them work.

The Life inside a tree is very lazy so it just hangs around and grows but the Life inside an animal just can't stop wriggling and jumping around

Life is the bit that makes...

Flowers want to open... Whales want to sing... and people want to watch T.V.

There is a Life inside every person and even though there are zillions of them each Life makes its owner completely different from everyone else

Life can make you so happy you just want to burst out of your skin with it or so sad you just want to curl up and sink into the ground

his whole book is about all the different bits of Life. t goes from before it STARTS to what happens when t GOES AWAY and there's lots of IN-BETWEEN bits as well.

The History of Life

History says that Life started millions of years ago when we all crawled out of the sea.

The very first bits of life were just dribbly blobs but soon they started to turn into animals

To start with there was only one sort of animal so everyone looked the same.

But as time went on we all grew different bits and pieces which would be useful for the separate ways we lived.

Birds grew wings for flying   Fishes grew tails for swimming

And people grew bottoms for sitting on

Everyone laughed at the animals who grew the wrong bits so they didn't last very long.

PEOPLE

people started by looking like monkeys. They went around completely bare eating bits of grass and showing off their bottoms

But somehow their brains got bigger and bigger and they made more and more inventions

Until at last they were brainy enough to invent trendy clothes, fancy hairstyles, fizzy drinks, burgers and pop music

HOW to MAKE a LIFE

First of all the Mum and Dad get together in a secret place in the middle of the night

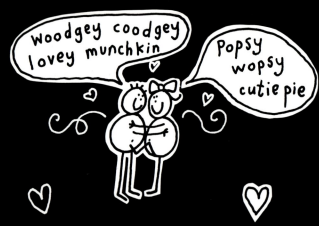

They cuddle and kiss for ages and say all sorts of soppy things to eachother

Then they put on their electric pants and when they plug them in there's a huge explosion and the Life just flies into the Mum

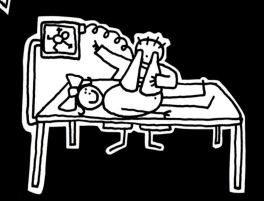

At first the Life is so tiny that you can only see it with a ginormous pair of binoculars

But if the Mum eats loads of grub and sings to it then it grows

The Mum then goes into hospital and the doctor attaches her to a machine which makes sure the Life has all the right bits

giblets ✓
brains ✓
tummy button ✓
toe nails ✓

At last when everyone is ready the Mum does the baby in her bed

a poem saying ↓

I Like You

You tell me I'm fat and I'm ugly
You tell me I'm utterly nuts
You tell me I burp and I fart
and I smell
But that's why I like you so
much

by Purple Ronnie

Friends

One of the things that makes life great is friends

shirlee Gordon me Maisy Nev

my mates ←

Even being very sexy and rich is useless if you haven't got friends

Because friends are what make things FUN

If you're feeling sad friends can take away your sadness

And if you're feeling happy friends can double the happiness

Friends can make all sorts of things worth doing that you would never do on your own

And friends can make everyday things feel like you're doing them for the first time

Friends can be nosey and friends can get you into trouble

t REAL FRIENDS are the smashingest things you can have

a poem for an

Extra Special Friend

If I had a million pounds
I know what I would do
I'd buy some extra special times
And spend them all with you

by Purple Ronnie

a shy poem

To Someone I Like

I sometimes find it rather hard

To say I really care

And that I like you quite a lot

But I've said it now - so there

hot flush

by Purple Ronnie

a poem about

Missing You

There are times when I really
                    do miss you
And think of you missing me too
So I close my eyes tight
And I daydream
That I am together with you

lovely daydream →

by Purple
Ronnie

OUR SCHOOL OUTING

One day the teacher said she would take our class to a museum and she asked us which one we would like to go to

explosions and killing

skeletons and people's insides

slugs and worms

But the girls won although their idea was by far the worst

please Miss could we go to a place that has pretty paintings and interesting things from history

yes shirlee what a good idea

First of all Teacher showed us some really boring pictures and she didn't even let us have ice-creams

Bored Girlie

This painting was done by ← a dead person from Italy

SOPPY SUNSET

Flick

oh isn't it romantic

Then we had to look at masses of pictures of flowers and people in the Bible and stuff

After that we went to the room of messy blobs and scribbles by trendy and modern people

one zillion quid

Then we found the expert who showed us a room that the teacher said was closed

nudie girlfriend lying down

look look they're all naked!

titter   smirk

Bare Lady in shell

and the nice man explained something to us

yes they agreed to take their kit off for the sake of art

fab

MAN WITH TINY DOO DAH

Naked girlies by the river

the expert

When we got back to school Teacher asked us if we'd had a nice day

She said one day our paintings might be in a museum

a poem about
↓
Exams

THIS is ridiculous
↓

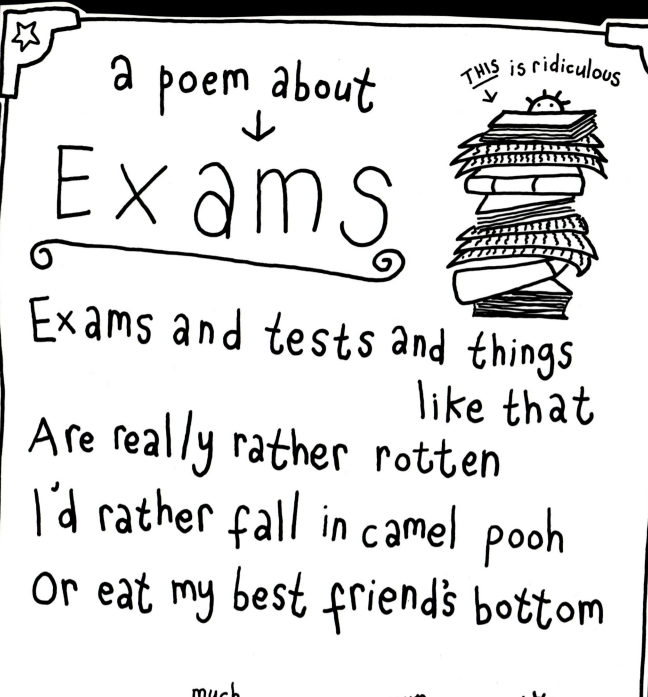

Exams and tests and things
like that
Are really rather rotten
I'd rather fall in camel pooh
Or eat my best friend's bottom

much better
↓

yum yum!

by Purple Ronnie

When the new teacher arrived she asked everyone to write down what they had done last term so she knew where to begin. This is what Nev wrote

The Tru Stori of Neville and the Monsta

Wen we were in histri ther wos a massiv growl and a Monzta wos piking up Shirlee. All the class ran for it exept Neville. THe Monsta wos qite scard of Neville and Neville mad a huge sHout and showd his mussls.

The Monsta puffed a huge fire but Neville iscaped and The fire landid on henri's desk and burned up his storiz buT the Monsta sed they wore useliss and anyway he DidnT bileev them

huff

fire

henri's Desk

BuT shirlee wos screeming and skweeling so Neville diD a commando aTtack on the MonsTa. FirsT he KiKEd in his Leg then he did a chinees burn.

The monsta trid to punch Neville buT Neville chargd out of The way and rammd the Monsta wiTh hiz Hed. Then he diD Massis of KArati oN the MonsTa and puT him in a harf NelsoN and choped OFf his Hed wiTh KUNG FOO.

blud→

The Monsta SErenderD and shirlee came crashiNg Down on top of Neville hoo wos compleTly fagd ouT. SHirLee gave Neville about a huNdred Kissis and Sed she luvD him wich orl the Clazz herd and Then orl the peepl Torked to him IN Brake and sed his styl of running wos brillant anD wen it wos gams the capTins pikt him Ferst.

THE END

Wise Man's Poem

Never hide your angriness
Or cover up your tears
But tell a friend you're feeling cross or sad
Cos friends are great to talk to
When your head is blowing up
And friends can help to stop you going mad

Keep your lips in practice
When you snuggle up with love
And have a hug each time you go to town
Cos every time you kiss someone
You top them up with Life
And when you don't they keep on running down

Laugh at any time you like
And giggle when you please
And let yourself be tickled without fuss
Cos when we laugh we tell the world
It's great to be alive
Which makes the world be friendly back to us

by Purple
Ronnie

Boys & Girls

At first boys think girls are rubbish but when they get older they start to think of them in a different way

As soon as boys begin to dream about hugging and kissing girls all the time horrid things happen to them

Their voices
go all wobbly →

Hair grows out
of their faces →

They smell and get
covered in spots →

But girls just get prettier and prettier

This means that boys have to learn tricks to make girls fancy them. Here are some of the best ones ↓

1. When you talk to girls, don't say too much about how amazing you are but tell them all sorts of things about themselves

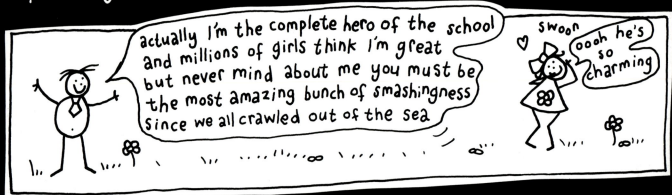

2. A very good trick is always to tell pretty girls you think they're brainy and tell brainy girls you think they're pretty

3. Always be as mysterious as possible

4. When you're with a girl, don't keep telling your mates how you think it's going

5. Don't show off about eating and drinking and making horrid smells. Girls don't like that kind of showing off

6. Quite a good way to make a girl fancy you is to pretend you fancy someone else

a poem about a smelly person ↓

Smelly

pong whiff

You take off your shirt
And your armpits are whiffy
You take off your socks
And your feet are all niffy
You give me a hug
And you're terribly smelly
Then you ask me to kiss you
— NOT ON YOUR NELLIE

by Purple Ronnie

a poem about

↓

SPOTS

a splatted spot

There's nothing wrong with having spots

In fact it's a wonderful feeling

When you line up a ripe one

Concentrate hard

And squeeze till it splats

← a ripe one

on the ceiling

by Purple Ronnie

a poem about

Bogies

They're snotty and gooey and dribbly
and green
They're slimey and sticky and
mankie
But I love gouging them out of
my nose
And rolling them up in my hankie

lovely

dig dig
gouge

life time
collection
of my
← bogies

← extra large
hankie

by Purple Ronnie

what is a Grown-up?

Grown-ups can be young or old or anywhere in the middle. What makes you a Grown-up is not how long you have been alive but how **IMPORTANT** and **SERIOUS** your brain feels. Here is a guide on how to spot them:

Grown-ups listen to music that doesn't have any words

Grown-ups learn long words so that people will think they are very important

Grown-ups are useless at making up games so they just stand around and say things

Grown-ups think business and newspapers are the most interesting things in the world

The Great Big Grown-up Hunt

When I went to Grown-up Land
I wore my best disguise
And Neville made a Grown-up hunting thing
Cos if you want to study them   blip
It must be a surprise
And that's the sort of stuff you need to bring

~

They never like to skip and dance   wheee
Or muck around and play   boring
They've always got their grown-up things to do
Like officing their businesses
And shopping things all day
And reading grown-up papers in the loo

~

They've even got a funny way   gossip chatter
of doing up their hair
The ladies paint theirs blue or pink or red
The gentlemen just lose it all
But make-believe it's there
By scraping little bits across their head

~

We tracked some to their bedroom
Where we got a big surprise
Cos both of them had taken off their kit
The gentleman was gurgling
And rolling round his eyes
But the lady didn't seem to mind a bit

~

He frolicked and he wriggled
And he bounced with all his might
But Neville said we shouldn't make a fuss
Cos interrupting Lady-Bouncing
Might not be polite
And we didn't want him bouncing round on us

~

When we'd done our studying
My friends all gathered round
And after thinking very hard I said
"Grown-ups are the curiousest
animals I've found
I think I'd rather be a ME instead"

by Purple
Ronnie

Bottom Burping

Bottom burps are one of the most useful and amazing things you can do

Sometimes they go off completely by mistake and at other times you can load them up in your bottom bit by bit and fire them out at precisely the right moment

Some of the best uses for bottom burps are:

making room in crowded spaces   embarrassing other people

& showing off to friends at Bottom Matches

Botty Language

Tiddler - shy and girlie with a little squeaky noise. Can only be done by tiny bottoms

peep

Whopper - warm and whiffy and fun to do. Great for talking about with friends

FLRP

Monster - noisy, smelly and only for huge bottoms. Wafts around on the floor for ages

FLURB

Trailer - slips out bit by bit as you walk along. Quiet and incredibly whiffy

FSSHHH

Rocket - the loudest of all bottom burps. Makes you jiggle and shake and almost take off

BANG!

One of the problems with bottom burps is people think the ones done by other people are rude and horrid and not half as good as their own

yum yum

whiff

a poem about
↓
Bottom Burps

PFFRT

↑ a
bottom
burp

If your BOTTOM burps in
public
Try to say in time
"Goodness gracious what
a whiff
It doesn't smell like mine"

me running for it
- having just
done one

PFFRT

Poo-eee   Poo-eee

by Purple Ronnie

a poem about

↓

Bottie Coughs

Why do people's Bottie Coughs
Smell of eggs and ham?
I wish they smelt of apple pie
Or scrumptious strawberry jam

eggy
whiff
FFRRP
Poooee
JAM 'O' FRESH

by Purple Ronnie

SWEARING?!

Swearing is great but it can be difficult to do properly unless you have had a lot of practice

Safety

First of all you must learn the rules because swearing can be very dangerous indeed

The Rules of Swearing

1. DO NOT swear at things that are bigger than you

2. NEVER swear in tight spaces

3. ALWAYS have a getaway route planned

4. NEVER swear at friends - even if you're only joking

Choosing Your Words

For the best swears you must choose your words very carefully. You often only get one good chance for each swear so you must not fluff it

Word Groups

Here are some of the best words arranged into groups

Surprise Words		Bottom Words		Noise Words
crikey	*	Botty	!	Crackle
Heck		Pants		whiff
Flip	◎	Willy	☆	Fizz
Blimey		Fart		Pop

Pick a word from each group to help make great swears. Practise with small swears first and slowly make them longer. You can even add some of your own words

☆ You **must** use the word "off" if you want to do an angry or rude swear ☆

Here is a Happy Swear

Here is an unhappy swear

If you get it right a good swear can feel smashing.
Here are some examples of where it is useful:

Getting Rid of Pests

Showing off to Friends

Frightening Old People

Getting Married

Getting married is one of the most important things you can ever do. This is what happens:

First the boy asks the girl's Dad if he will let him marry her. This is meant to be a surprise but the girl's Mum has normally found out first

The Dad always says yes — specially if the boy has got lots of money. Then he shakes his hand and tells hundreds of rude stories about him and the Mum

Then the Mum and the girl go shopping for millions of new clothes. They get fancy hairstyles and the girl buys a dress that is much too long for her

Just before the boy gets married his mates go out with him for a feast and they drink masses of beer and try to trick him into DOING IT with other ladies

On the day you get married you have to stand up in front of all the people in the church and the vicar asks you some questions to see how much you Love the other person

Then you must both make some promises of love which go like this

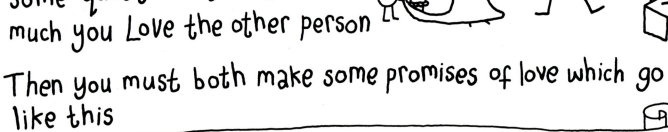

LOVE PROMISES

1. I promise this person that I will look after them forever, specially if they get very poorly.
2. I promise this person that I will not have rude thoughts about anyone else and that I will only ever DO IT with them _ever_.
3. I promise this person that I will share out all my private things like secrets, money and sweets.
4. I promise I won't get cross or giggle if this person whiffs in bed or goes to the lav infront of me because I love all the things about this person (even if they are horrid)

true love   sign↓ here

. . . .

When the girl comes out of church she throws her flowers up in the air and the first person to catch them will be the next to get married

After the marriage everyone goes to a huge party with Love Pie and Cuddle cake and such a saucy drinking potion that they all dance and kiss and happy around until the whole place is bursting full of Love

Right at the end, the marrieds drive off to a secret place with all their presents where they go to bed and get ready to love eachother for the whole of the rest of their life

a poem about

Getting Married

happy couple

It's all very well to get married
And team up as husband and
wife
But you can't ever <u>Do It</u>
With anyone else
For the whole of the rest of your
life

chastity
belt

by
Purple
Ronnie

a poem to say
↓
I Love You

When I am lying alone in my bed

All sorts of thoughts come into my head

Like why do I Love You as much as I do?

Then I know it's because you are You

by Purple
Ronnie

Grown-Upping

There comes a time when grown-ups have done so much businessing and grown-upping around that their muscles go all flabby and their bodies start spreading out all over the place

They get frightened that people will not fancy them anymore so they try to make themselves look sexy by:

showing off their hair →

running around in tight clothes ←

and showing off how much money they've got →

titchy pea

some of them try to stop eating grub which makes them very grumpy ←

and the rich ones just attach themselves to machines →

buzz suck tan

wobble

But being wobbled by machines is boring and not eating is the craziest thing in the world. Who cares about looking sexy when there's so much scrumptious grub and beer

a poem about

Pigging Out

I could take myself out for a jog every day

To lose a few pounds off my bum

Or work out for hours until I'm half dead

But I'd rather pig out and have fun

by Purple Ronnie

munch

Jammy Bun

pop

twang

creak

gobble

chocs

a poem about

Hair

You know that you are getting
old

And things are turning rotten

When hair starts falling off
your head

And growing on your bottom

hello baldy

← shiny pate

← hairy bum

by Purple Ronnie

us having a good squeeze

a poem about a

Big Belly

I like it when people have
bellies
That are lovely and cuddly
to squeeze
But not great big wobbly jellies
That dangle right down to
their knees

Jelly man

wobble wobble

by Purple
Ronnie

Old People

Old people are what you get when the most grown-up grown-ups stop trying to pretend they're young anymore. This means they can be as utterly barmy and loopy-headed as they like and everyone thinks they're incredible

The main thing old people do is gang together in clubs and go on thousands of outings

Old People Clubs

The Always Being in the Post Office Club

The Saturday morning club for selling cakes to all your friends

Differences Between Grown-ups & Old People

Grown-ups like storing money

Old People like giving money away

Grown-ups hate treats

Old People love treats

Grown-ups like fancy clothes

Old people like woolly clothes

...more differences

Grown-ups like big animals

Old People like titchy animals

Grown-ups like cold drinks

old pepple like a hot cup of tea

Grown-ups are always in a hurry

oldpeople don't care about hurrying

HEAVEN

When old people have had enough of living their Life flies out of them and whizzes up to Heaven

You can only get into Heaven if you have been good so there is quite a difficult test you have to do before you can go in

If you pass the test someone at the door gives you a ticket and it's just like a big Party where everyone floats around hugging and kissing and saying nice things to eachother

hey I really dig your hairstyle

God

The King of Heaven is called God and he's a very nice man. God is incredibly old and if you see him you must be polite and not tug his beard

God can see everything so do not biff or poke people when you think he's not looking

God

Don't try to hide
When you go to the Loo
Cos God will see
And he's bigger than you

by Purple
Ronnie

Heaven

Heaven's like a Funfair
Where all the rides are free
The clouds turn into bumper cars
And there's a hotdog tree

Everyone from history
Is floating round up there
Wearing girlie dresses
And flowers in their hair

God's in charge of parties
And his son brews up the wine
So all the folk can muck around
And have a splendid time